TUCKED IN FLOWERS

Hidden in Plain Sight

LORI KIRKLAND

Poetry by Lori Kirkland
www.lori-kirkland.com

Cover designed by Craig A Kirkland
craigkirkland@greatamazementworld.com

Printed in the United States of America

November 2024

ISBN 979-8-9916595-0-5

Dedicated to my husband Craig Kirkland for making it possible for me to write the happy ending to my life's story.
I love you.

lorikirkland

Other books by Lori Kirkland

Written and published by Lori Minutoli

Kaleidastorm (2016)
From My Heart (2018)
Released To The Wild (2019)
Emotional Bouquet- Wildflowers (2020)
Emotional Bouquet- Roses (2021)
Emotional Bouquet- Greenery (2022)
Emotional Bouquet-Filler Flowers *(2023)*

Written and published under pen names
by Lara Makanani and Hellion Saint

Poets In Love (2016)

All books available on Amazon

Links to each title on author website:

lori-kirkland.com

TUCKED IN FLOWERS

IN

FLOWERS

Hidden in Plain Sight

LORI
KIRKLAND

tucked in flowers

there are stories inside me
waiting to be heard
days
months
years
pass
as I watch them unfold
all while holding tight my soul
lips pressed
heart cold
stories remain
untold
you see
truth
is a heavy burden to hear
yet a necessary choice to share
so I'll traverse the unheard
and write in mysteries
I'll speak the unspoken
to finally be seen
without fear
I'll pen these lines
in hopes to reveal
just enough
my mind unkind
my heart unsatisfied
the stories inside me
are tucked in flowers
hidden in plain sight
I snipped them
arranged a bouquet
my beautiful truths
now on display

if flowers were my name

honeysuckle it would be
my name as a child
a drop of sweet innocence
grown wild along the streets
a burden to some
a fragrance to others
a delight still to behold
birds and bees drink from me
nature wildly nurturing me

english rose mirrors
my name as an adult
a contradiction
a misconception
soft and fragrant at first glance
robust thickness in hand
a wild and wavy flow inside
even though nothing aligns
a rose with beauty yet to unfold

the wrong fight

I don't want to be at war
with myself anymore
been fighting
far too long
stifling my greatness
for some weak-ass
self consciousness
the choice to change
has always been mine
to reject the shame and
break down the pain
but I was playing the wrong game
fighting the wrong fight
my image was never the enemy
it was just a trick of the mind
to hate my body
was the easy way out
the blame game no doubt
kept me from winning
it's time to change the game
no longer fight
I'm the mvp on this team and
the game is now called
winning at life

rewriting the story

the story I'd been telling myself
of failure and unworthiness
from broken promises and
unanswered prayers
to defeat and rejection
was a story I made up
in the grips of disappointment
like wisteria wrapped tree limbs
I held onto images of beauty
while slowly dying inside
my childhood ideals of
lemonade smiles in august
served on paper doilies with
powdered sugar cookies
too precious to let go
too sentimental to release
my expectations
a figment of my imagination
photos holding everything in place but
my heart
ripped out with shame and grief from a
fabricated fairytale
gone to pieces
the story I'd been telling myself was
keeping me from seeing
the story that truly is
a story of a brave girl
who kept striving for yes
no matter how many times
she heard no
who kept showing up
no matter how much
humiliation it cost
the story of a woman
void of familial affection

determined to embody
the love she yearned for
the story of a woman
who challenged
the stereotypes and norms
to curate a life of good memories
a woman brave enough
to weather the storm
also brave enough to then
jump ship to survive
a woman who stepped
out of a nightmare
and into her beautiful life
the story I'm now telling
not only myself
but the whole world
is the story I needed
to believe the whole time
this is my story
it was here the whole time

that august

my soul was tired
of being alone
yet I embraced
the solitude
travelled alone
great adventures
I did take
memories of a lifetime
I set out to make
photos for the gram
documented for the record
flowers to invoke
my emotions
displayed
yet unseen
self-love is an
intimate journey
I willingly took
in doing so
I discovered
a version of self
I've never seen
a beautiful soul
sent on a mission
discovered a new
purpose driven ambition
with pen and paint brush
by my side
creativity opened wide
my mind came alive
a desire to thrive
I'll always remember
that august I came alive

roses

roses I did paint
from poems I did write
a representation
of me
that felt right
little did I know then
what would come
to my sight
my name
also stemmed
from life
a rose
again
felt right

summit wynds

I came to this barn
expecting a farm
I had no idea
weddings were the norm
here in this place
filled with God's grace
wildflowers and sunflower fields
grown mountain side
I embraced and
basked in the warm sunshine
soaking in self love divine
on the day of my birth
I found myself worthy
to dream visions from above
the little girl inside of me
holding onto her dreams
of one day becoming
a bride it seemed
line by line I wrote it down
without knowing the future
I penned detailed lines
smiled while writing
wondering could it be
these visions were meant for me
indeed they were
those visions were meant for me

side by side

when poets cosmic collide
stars bright in their eyes
visions appear clear no glare
side by side studios
each a unique vibe
soundproof glass
the only divide
a writing space
an artist retreat
along side
a recording studio
this august vision
from the divine
will one day see light
no doubt in our minds
remember this poem
when you see us roll
greatness indeed
behold

write thunder

I am truth
I am love
in the face of adversity
I am rainbows
in a field of wildflowers
I resist defeat
I am powerful
I am greatness

to honor

at first glance it's quite simple
to hold in highest regard respect
look at her smile
know what she's endured
just to be here in this moment
know her joys and her heartbreaks
know that her indomitable spirit has
kept her on the rise never the fall
understand with love
accept without judgment
never cause any type of harm
to honor is to to recognize the warrior
to adjust expectations
know that life molded her
this woman is triumphant
worthy to be celebrated
acceptance looks like
forgiveness and tenderness
premeditated grace
understand and realize
the consequences of brutal
endurance has jagged edges
rough around the exterior
protecting the tenderness of
her strong yet delicate heart
honor sounds like a whisper
in a storm of adversity
a soothing verbal embrace
honor doesn't hurt
it doesn't highlight wrongs
it's not easily frustrated
honor makes her feel
seen   accepted   safe   loved

creation of love

I am the creation of love
not the hand holding
let's get married
frankie lymon
creation of love
not the big bang
here I am version
nor the blood-clot
stone boy version either
I am a grain of sand from
father abraham
a seed from a distant land
born here
with a purpose
I exist on purpose
at 54 I finally understand
what it means to
live on purpose
it matters not that I was
raised in dysfunction
rejected by people with
distorted perceptions
you see
seeds sown in neglect
still grow dreams
out of a crack
in the concrete
a rose
I am the rose
wounded but resilient
and ever so determined
to give love
spread love
and be love

though they reject me
I won't quit
say I'm not good enough
I won't wither away
won't co-sign me
I won't shrink back
my roots are anchored in
the rock
I have a purpose
their song remains the same
but I will appear with a new name
they will call me Rose
and I will continue the journey
fully focused
because
Lori by any other name
is still Lori

reflections in the sand

not a thought remains
no pain to be felt
just the warming sunshine
and soothing sounds of
waves washing over sand
wind whipping by my face
cleansing mind and body
a satisfaction unparalleled
by human effort
nature alone soothes
this soul of mine
sand unmoved
yet bearing
evidence of being
tossed at sea
how beautiful this image
drawing me in
to realize
the hard pressed life I've lived
brought me here
and now brings such
peace and joy to mind
what's been left
of each and every rock
tossed by the sea
now collects as
grains of sand for me

where you'll find me

perfect peace passes over me
oceanside as the sun begins
its journey beyond the horizon
blue-gray skies
clouds passing by
diamonds sparkle in my eyes
smooth movements on the water
gentle breeze blowing by
life and death on my mind
these diamonds transcend time
the mysteries of the sea
tell stories of love to me
romantic interludes
warm embraces
soft kisses
I want to get married here
when at last true love comes near
for by the sea I am complete
and better you with me
a honeymoon on tropical sand
to consume our love
underneath the golden rays
and moonlit skies above
ocean water the glue
that keeps me forever with you
in life or death
this is my place
here you'll always find me
for when I die
please put me here
as diamonds across the sea
each time you see the sparkles
you'll always see me

seen

earth
bears life
without
human touch
trees grow
flowers bloom
nature brings forth
its beauty
in solitude
a mighty oak
in draught
a desert rose
in isolation
lilies of the valley
a rose of sharon
a dandelion
without the touch
of man
as I am

inside

paint bubbles and peels
off the walls
the pressure too much to
hold back tears
my mind
keeps the heart
in safe spaces
rooms locked
without visitors
no traces
tears flow
it shows
this home
has never known
what it feels like
to be
home
to be loved
in ways that feel
comfortable
healthy
organic
mutual
endearing
you know healthy like
how love adds nutritional value
makes you feel better
than you did without it
organic love that needs
no gmos
no gimmicks
no mimics
no ordered responses
love that's mutual like
two quarters put together

equals fifty cents
times two is a dollar
which we stack
no putting back
or taking back stacks
endearing love
holding faces in spaces
embracing warm exchanges
these comforting ways
love
makes a heart a home
is foreign to me
it's unfamiliar
and I'm uncomfortable
wanting something
I've never had
I dream of a home
where love resides
inside my mind
I design the layout
I fill each room
with love's decor
a movie plays out
warms my mind
I visualize
hearty portions
of homemade soup
brimming with
acceptance and understanding
my senses fully aware
of the bounty before me
I desire to feast
at the table of your love
yet I know not which way
to serve or be served
I know not how
to fix a plate or
how to claim stakes
in the property of love

heart dreams

there's a place my heart roams
where roads are paved in
moss and cobblestones
where delicate blue flowers
cascade down stone stairs
where sunlight filters through
birch branches
cast lacy shadows on bistro tables
where wine glasses clink
and bouquets swirl
visions of rolling hills and
lovers gazing into the
landscapes of their desires
where smiles linger on
french pressed lips
and hands lay across napkins
holding the future in their palms
my heart dreams of salty effervescence
soothing every strain on my body
my mind dances in the
dreams of my heart
and holds onto every scene
like a premonition
an imaginary preview
of life yet to come
and I close my eyes
to feel the warmth
of the sun
of his chest
of his breath upon mine
you see the heart dreams
of something it can taste
and feel
and see
and it frees the mind

to escape
even so I believe
I believe in these visions
because I can see them
and feel them
this is my destiny
my desire to be free
and my heart full
and my hands held
and I
loved
to taste wine
on his lips and
sweets from
his fingers
to be held up
in reverence
and honor
in beauty and awe
to be the light and heat
and stars in his eyes
and dance
under the moon
as shooting stars of the night
my heart dreams in
pallets of royal colors
and of sparkles
in charming pastels
this place my heart roams
is my muse
and my heart
calls these scenes
home

I don't mind not remembering

because I do remember
the smell of lilacs on
the corner of dexter street and
west river road back in 1981
and the sweet taste of nectar
from the stamen of a honeysuckle
I licked in the same year
I remember how a softball feels
when you catch it in your glove
directly as it's hit from a bat
same year
and I remember the shadows
the oak tree made in my room at night
when I was a child
same year
I don't mind
not remembering things you
said to me last week or things
anyone says to me any time because
there's no way for me to remember
everything
maybe that's why I write
I used to think it was to help me think
now I think it's to help me remember
or maybe simply
to not forget too soon
I remember how it felt
to sit in the sun
feeling embraced and
loved by you and even
by the sun itself
before there was you
I remember many things
that hold no value
that bring pain

and remind me
of suffering
and for that
I try to forget
but why must I
try to forget
when I easily
don't remember so much
please know me
and know my heart
and know that
I tend to remember
moments
whether good or bad
I remember how it felt to be in them
in those moments
like moments in the sun
let's write poetry
and stories
and help me remember
for one day I may not
and then you can show me
or tell me
about the moments
and maybe
I will remember

my body feels like sin

it's carried my spirit
and housed my soul
for 54+ years
brought life into this world
and survived near death
many times
even so
I have hated it for as long
as I can remember
it didn't betray me though
it was the unkind and unloving
words of adults from my youth
what does a child know
but to think adults speak truth
today I brought it to the summit
and offered it as a living sacrifice
then baptized it in the early morning
dew and proclaimed
I am renewed
my body now feels like a temple
there is no longer shame in it
my body has been forgiven
all that this body has done
forgiven
nothing dirty remains
no condemnation
no judgement
no hate

this body

this body hasn't kept me from
doing anything I've ever wanted to do
it raised hell in college
endured an abusive marriage
pushed out two tiny humans
ran businesses
coached softball
played softball
planted gardens and
trees from saplings
fit on airplanes
trains and motorcycles
my size hasn't kept me
from any of it
I've been on skis
flumes and diving boards
this body wears bathing suits
lingerie
dresses and shorts
rocks work boots
flip flops
and high heels on occasion
you see this body
has never stopped me
from being active or attractive
they've swiped right and
filled my inbox
treated me like I was
beautiful and sexy
this body is flexible and soft
yet strong and tired
most of the time
it's not the body that I hate
it's something in the mind
that keeps telling me

this body is worthless
it's not a food addiction
that has me needing recovery
it's a mindset malfunction
that tells me I'm ugly
yet I don't feel ugly
this isn't a poem to
get your approval
but for me to claim self acceptance
I've achieved every kind of success I've
strived for
even being skinny for a season
but the mind has suffered
tremendous toxic exposure
from media
bullies and families
people in general
all who've been
exposed to the media
and families and bullies
I've never known total
body acceptance
but I'm working on it
I'm working on celebrating
not hating
achieving more greatness
not wasting time contemplating
my worth
this body won't keep me from anything
ever

redirected

I thought
I was going to write
about all the ways
we could love each other
without loving each other
I thought
I would tell you
what I wanted to do with you
and why
I thought I'd write
a romantic fantasy
and contemplate
sharing it with you
I thought playing
romantic wordplay
would be fun
because I wanted to
romantically play with you
with words
of course
however when pen
met with paper
my fingers only wrote
for me
not you
a love letter
from my heart
to my body
that turned the
axis of the world
on a new slant
everything I thought
swirled in my mind
and new thoughts
were revealed

you see God
intervened
on my behalf
he's making me whole
without lack
he's got my back
no turning back
I thought I was going
to write about you
but this story
is writing itself
about me

dark waters

she pours saline tonic into me
where fault lines burst open
and tectonic pulses collide
earth and sky divide
why
the stars unified and bright
lay atop the beast at night
why must it be fight or flight
why this night when everything
leading up to now was right
inhale the mist of mother's kiss
receive the splash on your face
salty salve to soothe your soul
she pours into me her saline
I hope to wake from this night

no need to tell

if you seek me
you will find me
a journey through
the labyrinth of my heart
discovered only by intention
there's no quid pro quo
no this for that
no asking while searching
you will find the answers
on your own
the questions you have though
will indeed determine your course
through my heart's maze
there's no need for me to tell
I've already spelled it all out
in ink printed and bound
you hold the answers in your hand
if you seek me
you will find me
though my heart
cannot be easily found

she gives

delicate blush ripples
atop sable water
a calm surrender
to nature's flow
moon beams glisten
anticipation
just listen
earth songs
serenade
sultry breaths
waltz
      step
            step
                  slide
rise
darkest silhouette outlined
as shooting stars fill the sky
she gives while waiting
for super nova to arrive

this right here is powerful

this book holds prophecy
words from God's word to my ear
straight to my heart
not the delicate part of my heart
not the this feels good to hear part
not the awww isn't that sweet part
not the kiss me right here part
of my heart either
when God speaks he speaks
to the guarded parts of my heart
behind the stone wall
I've torn down and rebuilt
every time someone got inside and took
a piece of my heart
you see
buried deep inside
past callused layers of bruised muscle
is soft embryonic porous tissue
there from creation
its purpose
love
it requires a genuine
selfless love
the kind of love
that penetrates
every layer
naturally
God told me
this love exists
he's been showing me
what it looks like
and he told me
it will be for me
I saw it clearly
this pure

honest
true love
filled the pores
of my inner sanctum
radiated light
beyond
my ability
to see how far
melted the calluses
healed the bruises
the stone wall
vanished
life unfolded
everything guarded
was set free
beauty
bloomed
from eternity
what's always been
meant to be
will be
he told me
it's for me

me

I am me
everywhere I go
it is my nature
to make beauty
out of devastation
rot
disappointment
rejection
to make a book
a fire
a verse
a decision
two sticks of wood
one fresh
one rotten
knowing
I am able
I took the
rotten
mushy
slimy
wet wood
singed it
the flames
revived it
without question
I took the lesser
because I knew
I could make
pleasure
deep satisfaction
knowing I can
knowing I didn't have to
knowing I did

sunny with a chance of flowers

yellow finches frolic
in fields of sunflowers
darting from flower to fern
bumble bees buzzing
busy between blossoms
while whispering winds
whisk by wind chimes
and I wonder
when will I learn to fly

offering

I don't know who you are yet
but I'm getting ready for you
I'm planting seeds
of tender self-loving care
that will blossom and cascade
flowing from my tongue to yours
you'll taste the tenderness
I lathered on my skin
you'll feel the gentleness
I required of my sin
as it relinquished power
and gave into forgiveness
the sweet tenderness
of the Lord's salvation
will enrapture your ideals
causing them to surrender
because freedom reigns
in weddings rings
in consummate exchanges
vows are the elixir
that release inhibitions
what once brought
condemnation
will raise a holy nation
seeds multiplying
ancestral blessings
when genuine love
binds hearts and souls
bodies become offerings
to God
I don't know who you are yet
but I will be ready
in God's timing we will be

let me hold you

come
put your head on my chest
let me wrap my arms around you
feel the warmth of my body
on your face
listen to my heartbeat
feel my warm soft lips
on your forehead
listen
everything's gonna be ok
feel my embrace
when you are weak
I can be strong
let me absorb your grief
let me soothe your anger
cry if you need to
I won't judge you
sometimes our hearts
become too heavy
they spill over as tears
I'll collect your tears
when they run dry
open your eyes
look at mine
you'll see me smiling
a rush of love will
cascade through you
we'll both feel it
your pain will turn to rain
showers of blessings

in my mind

I can only imagine
what it's like
to share the space
in my mind
with someone who's
not adversed to
journeying there
with me
so far
what it seems to be
is a lonely walk
for someone like me
I wouldn't change it at all
you see I've found
the way of serenity
not a follower found there
to pay any mind
to a girl like me
yet I have found the gold
in this solitude
I behold treasures
of countless kinds
not measured
by hands of time
nor valued
by droves of clones
these blessings
are all mine

I found me

I found me broken
and scattered about
a little here
some there
wondering
how did I get here
my mind
straight line set
since birth
on one
it was always going to be one
but one undone
turned to 21
turned to 41
for all I know
could be 101
anyway
one undone
and I'm torn
pieces of me not found
pieces of me
worn to the ground
I found me
fragmented
frustrated
frazzled
finished
and then I looked around
no one could be found
I looked again
and prayed
please dear God
open my eyes
shine a light inside
I want so badly to see

then I heard a whisper
there's beauty in the storm
beauty in the storm
how can that be
chaos and confusion
pain unbearable
my heart in agony
beauty in the storm
that's all I got
a whisper
beauty in the storm
like broken pieces of
colored glass and debris
in a cardboard tube
pointed towards the sun
I understood
a kaleidastorm story unfolded
opened up before my eyes
and bit by broken bit
the fragmented pieces came together
one healing image at a time
a story of lessons in
love and acceptance
of charity and compassion
I wrote my new life's story
I wrote every scene
I wrote the story I wanted to read
I am no longer scattered
discarded pieces of me
have been made whole
I found me
kaleidoscope art by design

kaleidastorm memories

I didn't go to work today
because when I opened my eyes
shattered images of dreams
towered over me
each one dancing as if
on tree tops swaying in the wind
I didn't go to work today
because when I opened my eyes
scattered images of my changing
emotions displayed as bouquets of
flowers on graves
        orange and yellows
        children playing in fields
        of blow flowers
        wishing their parents had
        more hours
        pink and purples
        teenagers by the river
        smoking and drinking
        carving names in forearms
        making out 'till dawn
the void too deep to fill
I didn't go to work today
then
I saw more colors through the trees
and realized
emerald ruby and garnet
were kaleidastorm memories
revealing the artwork of my life

love in action

in solace
I reflect
on those who
showed me love
not the ones
but the love
it is what I seek
the experience
of loving
inward and outward
the rise and fall
what man
can understand
the intentions
the actions
from mind
to hand
but the love
needs not
to be understood

memories

an unpredictable intrusion
on a sunny day
while driving to pass the time away
random clips of time long past
invade my mind
I hope these feelings
now stirred wont last
a door it seems to always open
like finding an old photo album
this trip down memory lane
not always welcomed
memories pop up unannounced
maybe they don't want to be forgotten
a piece of you from way back then
calling out to you now
a voice from the past heard at last
should we journey down this path
or shut the door and hear no more
I suppose it matters only
who's listening
you see
not everyone has an interest
if you should have some
who love to listen
draw the picture
set the scene
tell the story that keeps trying to be seen
memories are real pieces of who you are
not just pictures of where you were

who really cares

don't we just want our stories heard
I mean we don't want to tell people
but we want to tell the stories
we want to tell the stories because
they're so fucking hard to deal with
we want someone to listen because
we've been holding these stories inside
of us for years
nobody wants to carry
the pain that's required to listen
in order to listen
you have to hold words
you have to sit
in those hard moments
and feel what the person is saying
people don't want to do that
sometimes we'd rather not tell
because we don't want to hurt them
we don't want to put things in their
minds that they're not prepared
to deal with
that they don't know how to process
after all it wasn't something that
happened to them
so we hold those stories inside
and we hold the pain
and we hold the fucked-up-ness
and we just hold ourselves
I know I want to tell the stories
I want to tell the stories because
I want somebody to know
what I survived
I want somebody to know
what I've been through
I want somebody to say

hey Lori I'm glad you made it
I'm glad you survived
I'm glad you pressed on
I'm glad you're here
I appreciate you
I accept you
I want someone to care
about my story
and say thank you
for sharing that part
it's part of your history
and it matters
you matter

don't ask

when waves move violently
across the sea
fisherman don't ask the ocean
what's wrong

when the tide swells and crashes onto
their ships
they don't ask the ocean
what's wrong

when waves batter the shore and tear
down sea walls
they don't ask the ocean
what's wrong

when a riptide pulls everything in its
path under
no one asks the ocean
what's wrong

yet you and I are oceans
dwelling in flesh

we are in sync with the world

my heart tsunami swells
in response to injustices
internalizing rage against
the oppressors
pulling them under
to bury them at sea
they are dead to me

my anger stirs violence
that it cannot voice

don't ask me why
the ocean is enraged
why my opinions
slap you in the face
why my words
are heavy on your chest
just listen and observe

don't you see the people suffering
don't you hear their cries
doesn't your heart feel pain

I'm tired of explaining

I am an ocean
please don't ask me
what's wrong

f*ck them people

people with privilege
proclaiming Jesus
disguised demons
dressed in white
not pure white though
not pure like Jesus
no love given
no love found
putrid humans
rancid people
no salvation
no saving grace
repentance is foreign
to them foreign's a crime
what they see white as snow
we see stains far as the eye can go
if entitlement's a ticket
to get what's rightfully yours
congratulations you sick f*cks
eternity burns everlasting damnation
your final destination

Lord forgive me
your imperfect creation

mistaken attention

it feels good doesn't it
to be seen
to be read
to be heard
the words spoken on your behalf
elevate you
respect you
feed you
it feels good doesn't it
that's why you need me
my attention fills the void within you
and it feels good doesn't it
not to me
not deeply
if I'm being transparent it feels empty
don't get me wrong
seeing your smile feels good
hearing your laughter feels great
hearing your gratitude is appreciated
all of these feel good like
sun shining on my cold skin
or a breeze on my sweaty head
here for a moment of simple pleasure
and then gone
if I'm being honest
my attention is intentional
I mean to make you smile and laugh
and when I show up
I'm there for you
it feels good doesn't it
it feels empty to me

mistaken attention pt.2

you think I'm in love with you
and it feels good
yet you've mistaken my attention
you're not the first
they all assume
I'm in love with them
it's sad
I am in love though
just not with you
oh wait that's a lie
I do love you
exactly like I love
you and you and you
it feels good though
doesn't it
sometimes we settle
for a drizzle of love
we taste the sweetness
and rise with it
then we taste it some more
but just like a sugar high
that doesn't last
leaves us thirsting for more
we quickly learn
how to extract
intoxicating nectar
an innuendo here
a flirty complement there
the high returns and
we all love that ride
because it feels good
doesn't it
if I'm being honest
I am insulted that you think
I'm in love with you

yet you've
never enter the gate
you don't even know
where it is
I bet
you didn't even know
there was a gate
but that's your fate
not mine

a moment of darkness

sometimes
a storm cloud
appears
out of nowhere
even on a sunny day
nature is
mysterious that way
thundering and rain
falling out of nowhere
we accept it
as some thing
we cannot control
look around to the sky
for other dark clouds
hunker down and shelter
for the moment
once it's passed
we return to our joyfulness

lesson from nature
don't let one passing
moment of darkness
ruin a beautiful day

50 years is a long time to suffer

how do I
condition my mind
to not be affected by
the life I've lived
to not be affected by
the words I've listened to
to not be affected by
the emotional responses
I've had trauma from
50 years is a long time
to suffer other people
in just a few years
I've learned to love myself
I've learned to accept myself
for the damaged woman that I am
to accept myself with all
the bumps barbs and prickly parts
to accept myself for my harsh ways
and my brutal responses to humans
I've learned to accept myself
for my tender heart always
seeking to be loved
I've learned to accept
that my ways to feel love
are different than others
I've learned to accept myself
exactly as I am
and be proud of who I am
I've learned to accept
that no one knows me more
than I know myself yet
by sharing myself
and being transparent
others are at least able
to see me and

to see me
is the first step
to knowing me
how I condition my mind
is by realizing
I am not alone in this journey
there are many just like me
sharing is part of the healing
so here's to another 50 years
this time celebrating

triggered

I didn't see the train coming
not today
not in that moment
not when I was feeling
empowered
restored
blessed
I didn't see the train coming
never expected the impact
never imagined the possibility
never thought a good deed could

the intent was pure
without self interest
a charitable deed
delivered
received with gratitude
and then without warning
bam
words exchanged
my heart drained
my head exploded
the impact unstoppable
I couldn't breathe
I couldn't reason
couldn't listen
all I could do was
cry
ugly cry
ugly ugly cry
I didn't see the train coming
trauma response unpredictable

I'm okay
but I'm not
now I have to repair my heart
it broke in an instant
and that part of me
is not okay

my mind now wondering
if there were
any signs
any red flags
should I have known
or was this just
a triggered moment
something
I need to learn
how to deal with
I don't know
such is how life goes

holding onto the vision

these walls collapsing
around the fortress
of my heart reveal
a guarded stronghold
protecting a fragile
constitution
what once endured
in order to survive
now presents
outstretched
vulnerability
self made
determination
to display
wear and tear
as beauty
with grace
and strength
strong willed desire
to hold fast
the conviction
of God granted
visions
a future
awaits
this
believer
knowing
storehouses
full
of blessings
await

dry those tears darling

don't cry any more sweet child
your tears have no more purpose
when loving someone
brings you heartache
and repentance never comes
don't waste one more tear
you see those tears mean you cared
they mean you loved and lost
something wasn't right
and now it hurts
so learn from the tears
you've already shed
and please don't shed one more
you tried to love him
gave all that you had
somewhere he gave up the fight
and left you wonder what happened
let me tell you sweet thing
nothing you did made him stop
loving you
he made that decision on his own
your undivided attention is
too good for him
your devotion is too rich
some men settle for enough
some want just a taste
some want everything that's available
they are not for you darling
you are pure and lovely
destined for so much more
I know you have deep wounds
that show up when you're
trying to be strong
the consequences
of all you've suffered

but don't forget
your endurance
made you precious
tempered
tried and true
you are like fine gem stones
gold and silver
you are diamonds
never let them say you are less
if a man can look away
from your beauty
let him
if he can walk away from your love
let him
if he can shrug you off
turn his back and sigh
let him
you are worth
more than he can afford
you my dear
have treasures stored up
your value untold
no man has yet to know
the nature of your love
and you my tender heart
your loyal love is too pure
for the underserving
your love is special
old fashioned and true
save that for the one
who's breath hitches
when he sees you
who must gaze at you
when you are near
who clings to every word you say
and embraces every affection
you bestow him
let the one who treasures you
receive your gold

and please don't shed one more tear
this is not your battle anymore
this is nonsense and foolishness
leave it alone
let it walk out the door
and fret no more
do you hear me sweet one
no more

dry those tears darling pt.2

smile
and it reflects
back on you
laugh
and it will laugh
with you
kiss the one
who kisses your soul
and embrace
the one who holds
you with his attention
and his arms
love the one
who already loves you
without a doubt
you are safe and secure
in the protection of
a man who finds and protects
your value above all things
you are set upon the throne
of his heart
there are no tears
there is no crying
when you are loved correctly
he will have gratitude
for your love
not disdain
he will cherish and adore you

yes loved one
deep breath
you are worthy
love lies in waiting
hold your head high
release the disappointment

and learn the lesson
take the good
the bad
the ugly
as art of war
love is war
and you are still standing
so rise above this situation
soon you will soar

let it go
for all it is
give thanks for what it was
let it go
let the free bird fly and
don't you dare cry
you were made for something more so
explore
live free
love yourself even more

no point

I'm tired of trying to prove a point
I'm tired of illustrating who's
wrong and right
I'm giving up the fight
you can be right
been a
     long
           long
                long
                     road
I've grown tired and weary of words
words used as weapons
words taken apart
and put back together more clearly
words used to prove a point
there is no point
there is no point in being right
at the expense of being kind
at what point does one realize
we are all right in our own mind
I wish people understood
I wish people
never mind
there's no point

vomit

why bukowski
of all the poetry books
I had to buy his
love is a dog from hell
I hate it
the content
the imagery
the repulsiveness
of his tongue
his mind
his actions
but I read it
cover to cover
why bukowski

my poetry snitches

my poetry snitches on him
like mouthwash scented monologues
the morning after a bender
his over explaining
revealing his needy intentions
and I wonder
did he bend her
over explaining too

my poetry snitches on her
like body spray and dry shampoo
4am dunkin's drive through
when memories of orgasms rise
like acid reflux I wonder
does she swallow it down
or dismiss it
knowing it's all lies

my poetry snitches on me
like sunday morning confessions
fingers crossed
eyes open
looking all around
and I wonder
does he know what's
written between the lines
and the lies I've neglect to confess

safe space

a heavy heart needs a place to rest
worn from the weight of
loving unconditionally
exhausted from
misunderstanding marathons
this heart made of discarded tissues
exposed to razor blade word bombs
the mannequin weeps
with each heartbeat
shrapnel etched journal entries
upon flesh
trying to white tattoo blend on skin
don't look at me when I cry
x-ray visions of actions
reveal malignant tendencies
tied to travesties
a sorrowful sojourner
sporting silver linings
medals of honor
in place of inheritance
a weary soul needs rest
a safe space to decompress
receiving eyes that warmly embrace
soft acknowledgments
massaging memories
mouths muted and tongues latched
safe spaces are void of responses
welcomed flood of emotions draining
blood sweat and tear stained
broken vessels
deep anchored burdens
safe spaces are
faces without expressions
arms without frustrations
attention undivided

safe spaces remove
fear of rejection
cast aside all judgement
reserves advice until requested
if requested
safe spaces are filled with acceptance
hold space for understanding
even if not understood
space is kept safe
speak your heart out
release what needs to be said
sit in silence
breathe
again
now rest
heavy
hearts
need
rest

call me when she's dead

I found a crack pipe
under her tv last night
hidden in plain sight
first it was the blue straw
cut down to size
coated in white powder
then the glass plates
coated in white powder
the spoon
baking soda
the plastic health insurance cards
how ironic because now
she's in the hospital
I was cleaning up after her
in her absence after the stroke
but now it all makes sense
this senseless act of foolishness
now makes sense
the broken ornaments on the floor
the christmas tree as well smashed
the empty beer cans
and half eaten grinder on the table
911 for a stroke was probably
a bad high
I stood there last night in disbelief
the pieces I've seen all along
now adding up
now I know where the money was going
and why there was no food
and why he doesn't clean up after
himself
and why they
ewwww never mind
I stood there in shock and
suddenly I'm eight years old

and I don't know what to do
everyone's snorting cocaine
and I'm serving them soda and chips
and then I'm 46
and johnny's smoking crack
through a pen
and cooking it in his kitchen
and now I'm 53 and
standing in front of her tv
wondering why
why she couldn't just die

sad reality

mom
why did you choose drugs over love
why was I never enough
when I showed you how good it felt
to be cared for and
showered you with kindness
you beamed with delight
always surprised by how it felt
you were grateful in those moments
but they never lasted
like a drug high you begged for more
I never looked at it that way then
but I see it clearly now
you have always been rejected
from birth you were not selected
and even though they chose you
it wasn't enough
you were shown a different way
so you ran off to play with him
who would become my dad
you both lacked in love
so you both sought drugs
my whole life has been stained
by your quest for that unnatural high
the years I spent trying to
earn your love
trying to experience that high
I thought came from being loved
my whole life I've tried to be loved
to feel love
to be chosen
and to this day
you have chosen drugs over love
I still think about you mom
but now it's just in passing thoughts

over a year has passed
since we've spoken
no joke
it's the saddest reality
I wonder daily
if you achieved that ultimate high
checking obituaries
and bank statements
to see if you're still alive
it's mother's day mom
I assume you're un-alive
sad reality

the accounting of forgiveness

holding onto bitterness
recalling every offense
itemizing negative transactions
highlighting every mistake
correcting every error
emphasizing misspoken words

these are toxic fissures
allowing infractions to
form into infections
resulting in failures

you cannot build anything
while simultaneously tearing it down

imperfect people processing
piles of polluted propaganda
while making feeble attempts
to filter files from frontal lobes
is futile and serves no purpose
fueled by fear fatigue and frustrations
equates to failure

we are fluid and flow in and around
obstacles and barriers but
word bombs betray breaths when
bursting on broken halos
bitterness and brazenness
block every molecule from moving
forward towards freedom

the formula for freedom
is in forgiveness
there is no accounting of sin
no need to be right

at the expense of
someone else's undoing
forgiveness creates pathways
and removes roadblocks
forgiveness erases errors
and focuses on the positives
allowing the negatives to dissolve

pencil over the eraser's evidence
in the accounting of forgiveness
rewrite the wrongs into songs
smooth over the wounds with
an apothecary of words
turn mathematical accounting
into fine arts with mixed media
and melodies and metaphors

the accounting of forgiveness
yields magnificent masterpieces
masterful monologues
salubrious soliloquies
you see how beautiful that sounds

just forgive

vacant dreams

there's really not much difference
the house has stood alone
for hundreds of years
the empty rooms
the empty fridge
the unused yard
remains
I sit in it sometimes
everything remains the same
the faces change
but the story remains the same
sip some tea
remember dreams
realize this too shall pass
onto the next generation
with dreams
I hope they find a way
to let love live within these walls

in loving memory

sometimes I wish
I could be with you again
I miss seeing and touching you
every day like before
each day you showed me
something new to enjoy
every time it brought a smile to my face
it's springtime now and
I am reminded of you
your purple phlox edges
pretty pansy faces
buds swelling
leaves popping on branches
I miss the life you gave me
each day as the sun warmed the soil
dried up the morning dew
an emerald blanket for my feet to rest
blossoms for my dreams to grow
I think of you as I pass by others
and smile remembering
how happy we were
I don't know
if I will ever have that again
so for now
I memorialize you
with this poem
a tribute to my yard

what happens to the love

when you give someone your love
and they betray you
what happens to the love

when you love different people
throughout your life
and then they're no longer there
what happens to the love

does love rebirth
recycle or reuse itself
does it regenerate
or does it simply regrow
once it's dead

I've heard it said that each time
you love someone
you give a piece of your heart away
which left me wondering
how much do I have left
how much of my heart
am I operating on

I've also heard it said
that love is like sunshine
it is enough to reach everyone
at the same time
that leaves me thinking
how a new day dawns each morning
fresh sunshine every day
is love like that
a nurse once told me
that our hearts don't actually do anything
but pump blood

she said it doesn't control feelings or
emotions
I was taken back by this
so I read up on it and learned
love comes from the frontal lobe
of our brain
imagine that the brain
which houses our mind
is the central processing unit
of our love
am I now to believe
that love is a matter of my mind
is it mind over matter
or circumstance
or situation
do I just renew refresh
or reboot my brain's files
in order to love fresh and new
what happens to the love of old
I suppose it matters what
my mind is told
for some it's delete and repeat
for some it's saved on the hard drive
never to be forgotten
I've come to believe love comes
for a season
I'm hoping this is my forever season

masquerade

some would say
you're my muse
many however have abused
that word
trying to disguise lust
in their eyes
but not I
I have not opened the door
to my desires
my eyes are not hungry
yet my mind is feasting
so I firmly take hold
of this creative freedom
to write without fear

it is your face in the camera lens
your stage presence at the mic
your spoken word form that
indeed inspires me
so call it what you will
you may be my muse
so I will write fire from
my finger tips
in hopes that
words will gush
and I will glow
and then you
you will know
exactly what part you played
in my poetic masquerade

deep thinking poets

because we feel deeply
we share deeply
unlike the flow of society
where casual is
considered normal

casual conversation
superficially satisfying

casual sex
physically satisfying

casual encounters
egotistically satisfying

all normal

we the thinkers
our soul's depths
passionate

passionate conversations
intellectually satisfying

passionate sex
spirituality satisfying

passionate encounters
mutually satisfying

our normal

in just a few weeks
we've surpassed
normal

in just a few weeks
we've embraced
possibilities
unavailable to
the normal
in just a few weeks
we
well
we have become
and are still
becoming
something
extraordinary

that moment

they'd been talking
been knowing
poetry been flowing
on a mission
she wanted to see
needed to feel
to see if it was real
he knew the look
knew what it took
he held her tightly
precisely
made sure she knew
still she asked
and he replied
a gentle kiss
upon the lips
their hearts opened wide
they realized
God replied
after all these years
that moment in the sun
a new chapter begun

a moment in the sun

wrapped
in a moment
in the sun
his arms gentle
yet secure
around her
his acceptance
covering
her insecurities
her body anxious
on alert and
highly aware
closer
he pulled her in
his face
touching hers
his breath
in her ear
she is held
she is loved

make love to my heart

before you touch my body
make sure you kiss my heart
it lies naked inside of me
exposed in the dark
find her
and you find me
I am she
and we
need thee to
explore here first
before you traverse
the hills and curves of my body
before your fingers trek
this hallowed land
let your words wrap around my heart
as if held safe in your hands
assure her that your words are true
that you honor and respect her too
pour into my heart before
you pour into my body
take nothing that isn't given
and give as if an offering to God
for this my heart and my body
God created in love as an offering to you

cause me not to sin

he went in unto her and
she became his wife
as it is written
in the scriptures
a man
and
a woman
joined
became
one
that's it
no dates
no proposal
no ring
they did the thing
and a thing they became
please
lead me not into temptation
but fulfill Godly convictions
cause me not to sin by entering in
understand this
in order to be blessed
by the Master's hand
you must first take mine
be my man
as it was then
it shall be now
let it not be
the sinner's prayer
let's make a vow
to God be the glory
you may enter now

romantic visions

honeysuckle sweet sonnets
dripping from lovers lips
savoring similes
swirling in our hips
odes on fingertip scripts
dance up and down and all around
choreographed quadrilles
writing poetry that feels surreal
breaths hitch as prose rise
stars collide between our eyes
while whispering water colored words
we long to no longer hide
inhale exhale lilac soliloquies
orchestrate sweet melodies
desire a symphony of seduction
rehearsed verses reserved just for us
outstretched moon beams embrace
tighter as we gaze face to face
wisteria hugs within wantonness
while sultry sounds slide neck side
write us as cosmic celestial poetry
penetrate hearts and minds

forbidden fruit

one look is all it took
and she wanted that fruit
her mouth reminisced
of days long gone
when that fruit
made her smile
brought tears to her eyes
while on the inside
emotions stirred
caught in her throat
memories
caused a desire
to taste once again
that forbidden fruit
one look
and she took of it
all she wanted
her tongue explored
her mouth warm
her brain warned
there's supernatural power
in this fruit
power to overtake
power to shake
power to cause earthquakes
symbiotic undulation
experience sublime
when she wakes
please don't wipe the
smile from her face

holding on

moments in the sun with you
a soothing balm to my scars
your tight embrace
warm breath upon my face
a strong shelter in a world
full of disgrace
I escape the destruction and
am safe in your protection
the slightest shift of the earth's axis
a misaligned malevolence activates
atmospheric altercations
winds ever changing direction
a reflection of our intentions
do you hold onto what moves you
or
do you move to what holds you down
when a tornado rips through town
cling to me as I hold onto you
never let me go
we are in the storm
we are not the storm
my love for you is real
it is solid
anchored
deeply rooted
all of my life I have been waiting
for you
a man with intentions set on high
higher than I can even see
and I believe
I believe in things I cannot see because
you
you have spoken things no one sees
but my heart recognizes these things
the deepest parts of me

see the depths of you and
there we are connected
the tornadoes will rip through
trying to destroy us
just know this
I am never letting you go
I will cling to you for life
the life I want to live
is with you and I as we
we are the tree anchored
in thee almighty God

love delayed

eyes set on the prize before us
our dreams soon to be fulfilled
two tickets to tomorrow's joy
signed on the bottom line
locked in 54 no more
sorted and settled
presenting mr & mrs at the door
a new name she will carry with pride
to herself she makes a vow
to write the story
she's wanted to read
with the ending
she's been waiting for
love's a process and will progress
even though it feels slow at times
the journey is the story of her dreams
with highlights yet to be seen
love delayed will be love portrayed
in every single scene

his presence

when he's in the room
I'm at peace like
a gentle flowing river
winding through the woods
soothing words wrap my
unrecognized fears in fleece
a blanket for my tremors
I didn't know these thoughts
would resurface
one word pulled the trigger
and I became unraveled
and he
he wrapped his words around me
his arms calibrated my breathing
my heartbeat set to his pulse
and I realized
I'm safe
I'm safe here and more than that
I'm loved
more than that
I'm chosen
when he's in the room
I'm alive with purpose
determined

my heart

when I first gave you my heart
you smiled with a twinkle in your eye
because you already had it
tucked inside your chest
kept safe next to your own
my heart held in a safe space
you busy yourself non-stop
your hands tap tap tapping
your respect spilling over onto pages
post after post video after video
love displayed on replay after replay
it's clear for all to see you love me

show stopper

rising to the occasion
he stood without hesitation
tall dark and oh so handsome
this man needs no invitation
his presence commanding
undivided attention
eyes locked
she takes hold of the mic
and begins her oration
her warm breath
seductively persuading
his approval
deeply focused
exploring his depths
her hands gesture
as she performs
spoken word
grasping the mic
spitting bars after bars
her audience enthralled
her first performance
of this caliper
with great amazement
he explodes
exuberant vibrations
she's now reigning
best spoken word artist
he crowned her
queen of his heart

poetry blue

I love you
the way
yellow and green
love black
the way blue
sparkles
on ocean waves
and in my eyes
when I look at you
I love looking
at you
poetry blue
will always
describe
my love for you
poetry
brought me
you
I love you
the way
yellow and green
love black

in need of repair

so many rooms
so many methods
so much offered
little refused
still unreceived
this wave of true love
too much for my walls
please help me repair them
show me how to receive
l o v e

traffic with you

I wish to stop traffic
while I'm with you
I'd step out of the vehicle
throw both hands in the air
whistle to grab their attention
listen here everyone
I'm with the love of my life
not at all trying to stir up a fight
but you people are ignorant
and you're driving like idiots
causing me heaps of stress
please slow the fuck down
and get off my ass
stop trying to move past
you're just being an ass
I'm sick of your shit
get off the damn road
can't you see
I'm about to explode
baby calm down
you play on repeat
maintaining your composure
from the passenger seat
is it the traffic I wonder at times
because when I'm alone
I typically enjoy the ride
then again I don't drive
straight into rush hour traffic
for a plate no lie
no place is a date for me
with cars lining the streets
I'd rather stay home with you
all snuggled up in the sheets
it's clear to me
the problem is me

projecting my frustration
on others I see
now that it rhymes
I'll fix my mind
to slow down
and take the time
to find alternate routes
and not stress my mind
we can find plenty to do
when it's just me and you
we can write rhymes in no time
just like I saw you do
freestyle poetry with me in mind
thank you for making
me smile all the while
I'm stuck in traffic with you

august 1978

I turned 9 years old
and you
you were just conceived
because
9 months later
you were born
your feet on tropical sand
mine on new england land
the earth held us
both in its grip
molded and shaped us
and sent us on our way
we both had our firstborn
little girls
and our second born
little boys
both grew with moral integrity
values and perseverance
no matter the obstacles
in august of your 44th year
just as I turned 54
we grew closer
planted seeds of purpose
until upon a mountain top
we set our intentions
we decided
let's do this
so we became
mr & mrs
as it was written
back in august
poetry the catalyst
the center point
the axis on which
we became we

evening primrose

stargazing my mind's eye
the eve of cupid's mischief
a true miracle of the heart
to have a husband engraved
upon the flesh of my desire
a hallmark holiday to some
a routine tradition at best
but for me
my love is above greetings
in cellophane wrappers
tied in ribbons and roses
my love is evening primrose
nurtured by the sun all day
blooming as darkness makes way
a healing for the fickle and faint
the first to greet daybreak
love's one of a kind fragrance
one and only him on my mind
extraordinary as the earth spins
revolutions around the sun
infinity cannot be undone
we will rise like the sun

love on the brain

warm and sultry eyes
gaze upon her
this moment surreal
back in time these were
mere words penned in prayer
a vision from God declared
this particular man to her
a poetic dream come true
every detail
every desire
manifested truth
his warm mouth
upon her neck
his tongue
scripting scenes
whispering words
she longed to hear
they stare deeply
into each other's eyes
into their future
and every sunrise
love on the brain
and on the rise
caught her by
surprise
but that look
in her eyes
told him
no lies
their connection
met with blissful
inflection
sweet sounds
reverberate
the whole earth shakes

that's how they feel
each in the other's arms
the Master's plan defies
the strength of man and woman
forgive her greed
for she now craves
this love and attention
from her God given husband

sand stone

grains of sand
on distant land
destined to be grand
remain on shore
with hope
in their heart
waiting for
a new start
my heart filled
over spilled
family grows
part of my life
now feeling
complete
soon upon
this land
we will meet
turn sand
into stone
and build
a home

dadda's smile

in his voice
I hear his smile
joy in his heart
an ocean of love
miles wide
no matter
how far we are
this man
the strongest root
a constant
source of life

mother's song

she greets me with a song
her heart rooted and strong
to God she is forever true
her faith solid and lifelong
though miles away
her arms long
her embrace
through prayer and song
comfort me
her love warm

sisters laugh

many there are
a beautiful array
like sunshine
on a cloudy day
each one unique
fun loving vibe
sisters form a
powerful tribe
converse with
their brother
amuse one another
burst into laughter
smiles they're after
love runs deep with
laughter they keep
strong connections
in tact that's a fact

rastafari love

bredrin he says
these men and he
a sacred bond
I see
I and I
now understood
one love
clear to see
welcome me
with distinction
something
new indeed
sister
empress
queen
they say
with all
sincerity
levels of
respect
and honor
in everything
they do and say

unstoppable

when you know
you know nothing
can stop the flow
no poems rehearsed
no spoken word shots fired
they miss every time
love inspired minds
now pen rhymes
that will sweep up
dusty timelines
let me paint you a picture
to get your mind right
there's no comparison to
what mission we're on
our stage orbits the sun
our audience global
joins hands
lifts hearts and voices
in unison
you'll see one day
love paved the way
this the kind of love
we live on everyday

the jamaican poet

I've never once wondered why
I was the lucky one to catch his eye
why I was blessed to join hands
with this amazing man
you see long before we understood
that we were meant to be
our journeys aligned supernaturally
poetry brought him to my door
but my vision soon discovered
he was so much more
than what he presented
on the stage floor
deep inside of us
at the core
our hearts are woven
together like never before
love takes us places
meets faces and leaves
traces of greatness
everywhere we traverse
living poetry unrehearsed
our lives designed divine
until the end of time

Mr & Mrs Kirkland 2023

Lori Kirkland 2024

the author

Lori resides in Rhode Island with her husband Craig. She is the founder of Pawtucket Poetry, where she connects poets with safe spaces to share their poetry, hosts open mic events, and supports emerging spoken word artists as they courageously begin to share their poetry.

In addition to writing, she enjoys nature walks, scenic drives, and loves collaborating with her husband on creative endeavors. Lori hopes to one day have all of their children and family members around the table for homemade Jamaican meals with fresh cut flowers and herbs from their own gardens.

Lori's books are easily available through her website or by emailing for a signed copy.

www.lori-kirkland.com

lorikirkland11@gmail.com

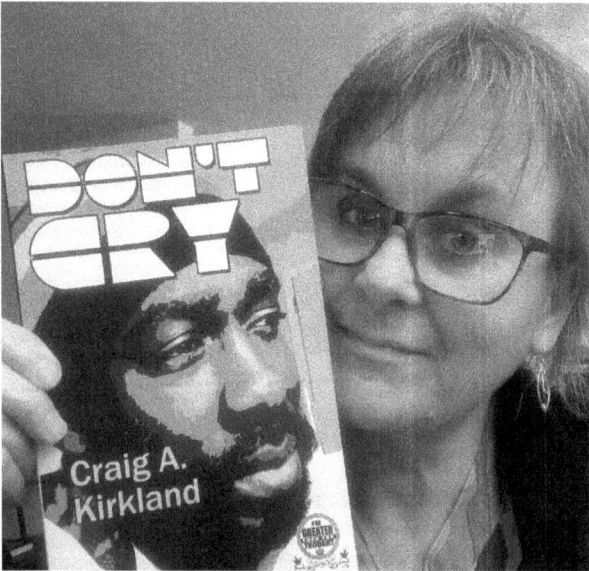

the muse

Craig A Kirkland aka Amaziyah The Great is the author's husband and the inspiration for many of the poems in this book. The two met at a Pawtucket Poetry open mic event.

The Jamaican Poet, the Rhode Island Icon Award winning short movie, was created and produced within 48 hours by Craig Kirkland for the 2024 PVD 48HR Film Project. Actors forming *Team Great* came together from Rhode Island and New York with supporting voice actors from Spanish Town, Jamaica including Craig's children **Ny Ashia** and **Ajani Kirkland.** Lori Kirkland assisted in filming the movie.

Craig A Kirkland's first book of poetry *Don't Cry* is available on Amazon or if you're in the continental US you can get a signed copy by contacting him directly via any of the resources listed below.

Amaziyah The Great is a multi-talented Jamaican who not only writes and performs   poetry but is an artist, author, film maker, actor, song writer and singer. His poems and music can be found on all streaming platforms.

His company **Great Amazement Multimedia Entertainment LLC** offers photo and video services including: music videos, short films, tv/radio commercials, album art, flyers, logo designs, party ads, social media promos and much more.

Connect with Craig on any/all of these platforms:

YouTube GreatAmaziyah

X @preciselygreat

Instagram @preciselygreat

Instagram @greatamazementworld

Threads @greatamazementworld

TikTok @artistcraigkirkland

FB Amaziyah The Great Music

FB Amaziyah The Great Collections

Amaziyah The Great 2024

GREAT AMAZEMENT MULTIMEDIA ENTERTAINMENT LLC
"Great way is the gateway"

PAWTUCKET · RI
Pawtucket Poetry
EST. 2020

O